DON'T GO VIRAL

The Video Marketing Growth Path for Startups and Entrepreneurs

By Dan Englander

SalesSchema.com

ISBN-13: 978-1516998784

ISBN-10: 1516998782

Table of Contents

1. Getting Started

You were probably raised by video—movies, television, commercials, that PBS special your teacher played when she was hungover. . . . After massacring the puny radio star, video became the effective medium for marketing anything, from lofty political ideals to cheap blenders.

At the inception of the internet, technical and inspirational hurdles made video take a backseat to static content like text and images. However, in our age of YouTube, compression advancements, and a milieu of content sites, video is back where it belongs, enjoying unsurprising dominance.

I know I'm telling you things you already know. If you're involved in marketing or sales, even on a minor level, you're probably enduring a constant barrage of facts, figures, and demands to invest in this space: *1-minute of video is worth 1.8 million words* — Forrester Research; *100 million people watch video everyday* — Comscore; *Blood-Drenched Berserk CEO Demands More Web Videos* — The Onion. Newly-launched startups have made over $50 million in a matter of days from the simple act of adding an explainer to their homepages (you'll learn more about this later).

With all this potential, you might feel like you're under pressure to dive headfirst into this environment by launching a campaign. Guess what? You *should* feel some fire under your seat. Video has the potential to be your most lucrative marketing asset.

That being said, there's no reason to be hasty or less-than-strategic. After all, if you have a new product or service, your time and resources are probably limited. In addition to overspending, there are two outcomes that are out of the question: creating mediocre content, and/or failing to meet your objectives. The stakes are just too high; video is seen and shared before any other content.

I've worked with a multitude of tech startups, Fortune 500s, and other companies to create over 100 marketing videos. As the first employee and Senior Account Manager at IdeaRocket, a New York-based animation studio, I had the privilege of bringing in business and managing productions for clients like Venmo, Electronic Arts, Showtime, and around a dozen Fortune 500s. From these experiences, I've developed some observations that will come up throughout the chapters. A big one is that companies tend to lose sight of the forest for the trees. Video has so much potential, and quite many moving parts. For this reason, creators often fail to take a step back and answer the simple and important questions: *To whom am I speaking? Where will my video live? What is the next action my viewers should take?*

I wrote this book to help you achieve your goals by envisioning and tackling video marketing the right way. By the time you're done, you will have the framework for a campaign launch plan. You will have a reasonable target Return on Investment before you take the risky financial leap into production. You will learn about all sorts of underused, memorable, and cost-effective formats. And yes, we'll get into the nitty gritty; you'll gain access to all sorts of distribution strategies, tools, and hacks. Above all, you will head into this unruly landscape with a roadmap.

Resources

This is an analog and quasi-digital text on a 100% digital topic: How the hell are we going to make this work? Why with a resources page, of course!

Throughout the book, I reference "**Resources**", including tools, spreadsheets, downloadable documents, and other goodies.

When you get to your computer or mobile device, please go here to get access: **SalesSchema.com/Video-Marketing-Landing.**

To get these materials, I'm going to ask for your email because I want to ensure you exclusive access. More importantly, you'll receive our newsletter, which is the best way for me to keep you informed about this evolving space. Continual learning is important so you can leverage new strategies, tools, and hacks. You can opt out anytime, and I promise I won't flood your inbox.

The Growth Path

You might be wondering what comes when. Let's talk about the order of things by checking out the Growth Path diagram below.

By the end of this book, you should have the know-how to hash out almost all of Phase 1: Strategy. You will get your ducks in a row so you can launch your campaign with ease. Your strategy will encompass aspects of execution: Production, Launch, and Measurement.

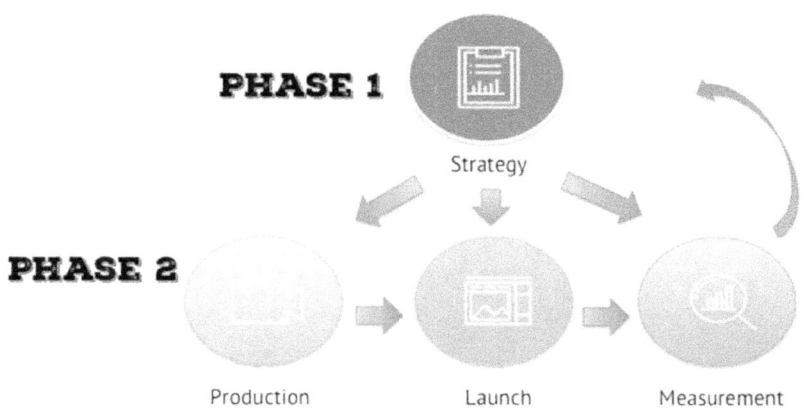

I laid everything out in this order so you can create a better video. I've seen too many companies throw their weight into productions   without developing a clear path forward. You'll avoid a ton of headaches, save time and money, and get dramatically better results by planning a little.

Your production plan deserves undivided attention. It will cover script writing, voice over, technique, producer selection, and other moving parts. You'll learn about these areas and many more in the sister book, which you can find at the below link. It focuses on explainer videos, but the strategy is applicable to almost any format.
SalesSchema.com/DanAuthorPage

Down the road, once you have created and released your video to the world, you will measure performance using monitoring tools like Google Analytics. With the squiggly arrow, you will iterate, using the data to inform how you showcase current and future campaigns.

2. Goals and Vision

What exactly can you hope to accomplish with this medium? Let's talk about it. . . .

I know I just got done complaining about the video stat barrage, but I want to dig into the data-driven reasons to spend your time on this medium so you can get inspired by its potential.

- 85% of people are more likely to buy after watching an explainer or a similar product video (Video Rascal).
- 71% of marketers say it converts better than any other content (ReelSEO).
- 1/3 of all online activity is spent watching video (Digital Sherpa).

The cold numbers aside, this medium will help you explain your offering. It will make your product or service approachable and understandable. It can condense a huge amount of complexity down to a few moving symbols and voice over phrases. Lets look at a multi-million dollar case study.

The Dropbox Explainer

The original Dropbox explainer is the grandaddy of them all (check it out in **Resources**). It helped popularize the explainer video genre. You might know Dropbox as the cloud storage leader, but there was a time when they were new and fledgling. Switch Video, their producer, provides these findings:

While competing with dozens of similar storage companies, Dropbox managed to grow from 0 to 100 million users within five years. At first, the company used Google Adwords to generate traffic, but soon found this option too costly: They were spending up to $388 per customer while selling a $99 product. To go a different direction, they launched a viral referral campaign, encouraging users to share invites in exchange for additional storage. The campaign was a hit, and they garnered over 2.8 million invites within one month.

Dropbox went further. They focused viewer attention almost 100% on their 2-minute homepage explainer. Aside from the video, there were few clickable options. The simple, minimalist explainer communicated an immense amount of complexity in very little time. The result was a 10% increase in signups, or 10 million additional users. At a value of $4.80

per user, that's an extra $48 million (while spending nothing on advertising).

In competitive verticals like cloud storage, the winner usually touts an awesome product, as is the case with Dropbox. When it comes to complex offerings, the victor must also make their message easily digestible. A well-composed explainer can accomplish this, but a mediocre piece can make things more confusing.

The Dropbox case study demonstrates what to do right— not just in terms of the content of the video, but when, where, and how you showcase it. We'll dig into these questions before long.

Maybe this example looks like it's out of your league. After all, we're talking about one of the most successful consumer software products. But I encourage you to keep an open mind. Focus on that 10% conversion increase: What would that mean for your offering in the long term? In a later chapter you'll learn why this gain is conservative.

Video and Your Funnel

An extremely common mistake is assuming that your new site visitors are ready to buy. Marketers mess this up all the time, including yours truly. From working in sales and attending networking events, I should have avoided this mistake by taking lessons from comparable real life situations. For example, you don't meet a prospect at a cocktail party and immediately hard sell; you act like a human being. You introduce yourself, learn about their needs, talk about your product, and so on.

Your funnel is an excellent tool for visualizing your visitor's status as they approach your offering. Your funnel is bigger than just video; it should guide all your marketing efforts. Check out the below diagram.

The complexity of your funnel will depend on your offering. If you sell an $2 app, you might have just two stages: visitors and customers. If you sell a 5-figure enterprise software product, your funnel might have many more stages, like visitor, marketing-qualified lead, sales-qualified lead, prospect, customer, and repurchaser. Regardless, your goal is to turn strangers into customers by moving them down your funnel.

For our purposes, the big question is: Where and how should your video(s) fit into your funnel? The rules aren't set in stone, but different formats will fulfill different objectives. Generally, promotional videos should live at the top of your funnel. They will help turn visitors into leads. After leveraging a compelling call to action and acquiring their email address, you can nurture your leads with helpful content until they're ready to buy. This might mean providing an email newsletter, ebooks, whitepapers, and other tools.

If you're creating a long-form educational video, like a product tutorial or walkthrough, it should live further down your funnel. It will transition leads to a major next step, like purchasing your product or a 30-day free trial.

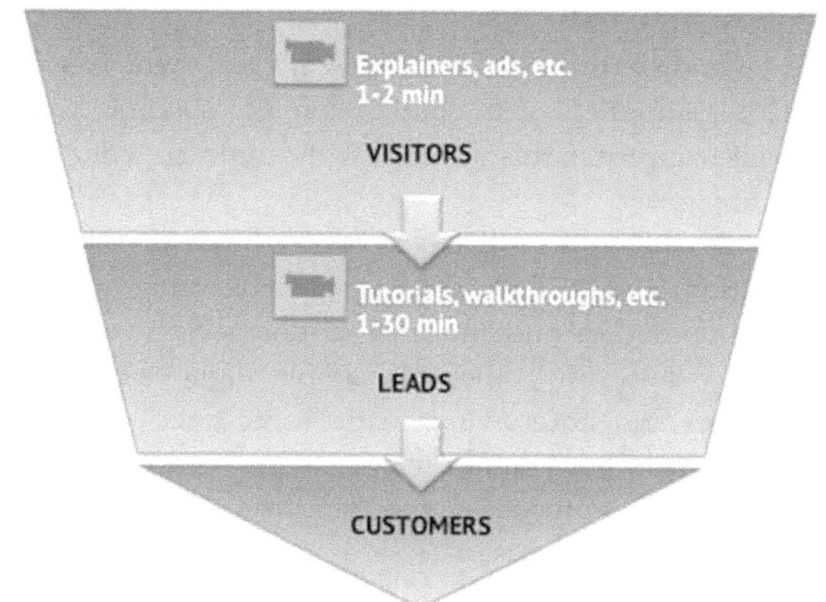

Explainers, ads, etc.
1-2 min

VISITORS

Tutorials, walkthroughs, etc.
1-30 min

LEADS

CUSTOMERS

How to Envision

With all the hype around video, it's tempting to adopt the "if I build it they will come" mindset, treating the medium as the end result. Instead, you should envision video as a tool, a powerful one at that, but not your final outcome.

Instead, your end result will be your overarching marketing goal. With that in mind, your piece should gel with your other initiatives. Later we'll go into all sorts of marketing ideas and tools, as well as creating the foundation for your message. Before you're influenced by this learning, start to think of ways you can incorporate video into your current strategies. Chances are your intuition will be spot on. Simply answer the following question: "What are 5 ways I can incorporate video?"

Identifying Goals

While avoiding the *Field of Dreams* fallacy, here is where you'll get specific about your vision for success. Many companies approach this medium with vague, convoluted, or conflicting goals.

Going viral, for example, is a vagary (more on this later). In addition, I've talked to companies wanting to target multiple audiences and multiple distinct objectives within one short video. A hypothetical example might be Etsy going after buyers and store owners at the same time. It's not an impossible feat, but you're making things hard on yourself. It's much easier to focus on one prioritized objective and as few buyer groups as possible.

With that in mind, below you will find the most common concrete goals. These are ideal because they can be measured. Take a second to decide which one is most appropriate for you at this particular time.

- Sales
- Conversions
- User acquisition
- Lead generation
- Audience
- Talent acquisition
- Engagement
- Education
- Communication

Making Sure You're Ready

We can accept that your product might not stay exactly the same forever. Invariably there are buyer groups you didn't consider, and additional features or tweaks. That being said, your offering should be at a sufficient level of completeness before you take the plunge into production. With that in mind, save yourself a migraine by answering these questions:

Are you still beta testing things? Do you have a pivot in your near future? Are you still wearing your development hat more than your marketing or sales hat?

If yes, then you should probably press pause until you hash things out, or until you're fully primed and ready. As you'll learn later in the <u>production book</u>, editing key parts of a completed video is usually more trouble than it's worth.

When to Create and Revamp

When should you create a video? When should you revamp your existing piece? I've heard these questions a lot.

Let's start with common milestones and conditions that might precipitate a new video campaign:

- New product or service
- New feature
- Event
- New audience
- Audience confusion
- Brand realignment

These triggers aside, you should make sure the stakes are high enough to justify the time and money investment. We'll get into this later in the ROI and Measurement chapter.

As for revamps, it will depend on your situation. That said, no video is completely evergreen, in the same way that no website should exist in stasis. Like your site, your video must reflect changes to your product or service, or else it will be misleading.

Beyond that, design and user experience trends change every few years, and your site has to evolve. Your video should evolve along a similar timeline. Generally, revamps should happen every 2-3 years for smaller sites, and every 5-7 years for large or enterprise sites, with smaller changes every 2-3 years.

Calls to Action

To move your audience to the next stage of your funnel, you should put a lot of weight into your Call to Action, or CTA. This is one of the biggest factors for getting results. Make sure your video does not fade to black, leaving viewers without an immediate next step. I see this mistake all the time.

When creating your CTA, go with clear language, and more importantly, simple actions. A common CTA is, "Contact us for more information"; or, "Schedule a free consultation." Although this messaging makes sense for certain industries, it's a tall order. Many marketers and salespeople assume that a few minutes of a prospect's time is a small ask. In reality, a "five-minute call", which invariably becomes a 15-to-30-minute sales pitch, is a major commitment for busy people. It's usually more effective to pursue that goal later in your funnel. For example, your CTA for bottom funnel content, like walkthroughs, might be a consultation request.

In most situations, however, you should make a small ask that pays off big in the long run. Examples include, "Download our free ebook"; or, "Sign up for our newsletter."

Make a point of grabbing email addresses during this process. I did this to you at the start of the book, so it looks like I'm giving you a look under the kimono! The old adage holds true: *The money is in the list.* Once you have addresses, you can serve your audience helpful content and get them to purchase.

Make life easy by automating email with the help of technology. You can use autoresponder services like AWeber or MailChimp. If you have the budget, you can go with a comprehensive marketing automation service, like HubSpot or Vidyard (learn more in **Resources**). Regardless, make sure you use technology to track user engagement at each point of contact.

If you keep your CTA top of mind from the get-go, you'll be miles ahead of so many companies that neglect them, or feature unreasonable, low-converting requests.

Landing Pages

Most likely, your website's landing page will be your video's main residence. The Dropbox example and many others demonstrate this asset's effectiveness in this environment. Your website is your home, where you can immerse your audience and move them through your funnel.

Here are specific gains you can expect from making a video your site's hero:

- **SEO**
  Google stated emphatically that they prioritize video over many other factors in their ranking algorithms.

- **Conversions**

An immediate understanding of your product or service will drastically increase the rate at which you move visitors to the next phase.

- **Engagement**
A video is more likely to be clicked before any other site content. Once it's watched, viewers are many times more likely to access other pages. This means people spend more time on your site, and your bounce rate can significantly decrease. This in turn will boost your SEO.

Here are two key strategies for making video deliver on your landing page:

- **Make Video the Hero**
There are many ways to build a landing page. Platforms like LeadPages and OptimizePress are helpful creation tools. Remember that video should be your centerpiece. With the medium's potential in mind, make sure you don't squander its power by putting it in a strange or easy-to-miss place. I've observed companies featuring high-quality explainers as thumbnails in the sidebar, or on low-trafficked informational pages. The results were dismal.

- **Make CTAs Big and Obvious**
Viewers should not have to debate about what to do next. To make a clear CTA, use an in-video overlay. If you don't want to fiddle with that, then just place a big shiny button alongside your play box (check **Resources** to see what I'm talking about).

Keyword Research

As a ground rule, keywords and SEO should be an afterthought. Your top priority will be making the best video possible. The crawling robots must take a backseat to your human audience.

When it comes to your marketing strategy, however, roughing out your keywords is a valuable exercise. KW research will inform how your audience converses about your niche and the products and services surrounding it. Your research will put you in touch with your users' needs, challenges, and desires. Later on, your findings will inform your message and script.

KW research and SEO strategy is its own book. This section is meant to give you a primer and some tools for getting off and running (see **Resources** for links).

- **Google Keyword Planner**
  A tool designed for Adwords marketers, the planner is essential because it will tell you the traffic for whatever term you search. Google now requires you to set up an Adwords campaign before accessing the planner. You can get around this by setting up a campaign and putting it on pause permanently, with a budget of zero. This is an annoying hoop, but it's worth it.

- **BuzzSumo**
  A product from Appsumo, it measures the relative impact of different posts based on the keywords you search. It measures performance by social media shares. You can narrow results by focusing on a particular site or demographic.

- **Quora**
A sophisticated question and answer site, this is one of my favorites. By searching for a few intuitive industry keywords, you'll discover a ton of questions and issues your potential customers are experiencing. This resource will inspire great ideas.

- **Google Trends**
Once you have keywords listed out, you can compare competing phrases in Google Trends. For example, I might compare "product video" and "explainer video". Google draws from its all-encompassing index to show which term is more popular. A newer feature allows you to zoom in on certain channels, like YouTube.

To get started, plug in a few industry KWs, and before long you'll populate a huge list of terms. From there, prioritize the most relevant, well-trafficked words, and separate them into two groups: primary and secondary KWs. This list will be your source for future titles, descriptions, and metadata. More immediately, these KWs will go into your message and script.

Killing the Virus

As yet another client asks me to make their video "go viral", my facial muscles contort into a terrible cringe while I fight to maintain a professional smile. . . .

I'm being harsh. We're trained to seek virality with everything we create: photos, Vine clips, blog posts, . . . so why not marketing videos? There are a few reasons why seeking virality is probably *not* your best move.

For one, it's unrealistic. Asking for viral is like asking for a platinum record. Massively popular content has a certain implacable something that's only obvious in hindsight. You can analyze Old Spice or Dollar Shave Club commercials all day, but there are no guarantees that you will be successful.

Secondly, "viral" is a buzzword for "popular", and popularity is a vague goal. It's difficult to tie "popularity" to concrete business objectives. Big corporations and cat video filmmakers can afford to be vague, but if you have a new product, you can't. Instead, go for specific objectives like the ones we covered earlier.

With my gloom and doom warnings out of the way, maybe you have an awesome viral idea, and I'm crushing your dreams. Sorry about that. If you want pursue virality, make sure you're willing to take big risks. There's no success blueprint, but this usually means being extremely funny, provocative, or controversial.

After getting enough "make us viral" requests, I found that most companies are unwilling to do what it takes. Since we were rarely permitted to go out on a limb, we usually ended up creating explainers with a joke here and there: good stuff, but hardly viral material.

Also, make sure you don't have to close the loop between viewership and conversions. Old Spice, for example, reported a significant sales dip during the height of their viral success.

Takeaways

Video can bring massive results, but only if you drop the "if I build it they will come" mindset. Start to create your vision for success. Take the $48 million lead set by Dropbox and others and craft it into something something real and attainable. Consider the ways you can bring video into your existing marketing initiatives. Pinpoint specific goals, like conversions or sales. Consider calls to action from the get-go, an easy step that will put you ahead of most video marketers. Envision how this asset will live on your site, and how it will interact with your viewer's journey. List high-value keywords you can draw from throughout your campaign. With these actions, your end product will be stronger than ever.

But what should your video say? And to whom? You'll figure this out in the next chapter.

3. Your Message

At IdeaRocket, we created every one of our 100+ videos by starting with a 20-question discovery process. Our Creative Interview was conceptualized by our creative director and founder, Will Gadea. The questions aren't prodding. They're not going to pull out groundbreaking realizations about your product. They're simple, and at the beginning of each interview, I used to feel slightly embarrassed for asking such basic, assumable questions.

But simplicity is the point. This is a destructive exercise, in a good way. The objective is to filter out the stuff that doesn't matter just as much, if not more, than focusing on what does. One of the most common missteps is overcomplicating your message for the sake of sounding intellectual.

You already know what's valuable and intriguing about your offering. You know what your buyers want. There's no need to dig too deep for hidden gems. After all, you'll ultimately have to condense your message to around 90 seconds.

To set expectations, you might not be able to fill in the most complete answers from the get-go. Your technique and distribution strategy, for instance, will get more support in later chapters. That being said, it's important to start marinating on these considerations early.

If you're hitting a wall with these questions, stay tuned for the end of the section. You'll learn how to get answers by taking a few easy steps into customer development.

Product

These are the important questions you should nail down about your product or service. Most of these inquiries are specific to an explainer or a product video. If you're going to create a different format, like a testimonial or culture video (more on these in the next chapter), you should tailor these questions to those approaches. For example, if your goal is communication or education, you might think of your "product" as your idea or main argument.

Chances are you've been unsuccessfully sold a solution for pain you don't feel. Conversely, maybe you have looked to a product to solve certain problems, and their message pushes you away by focusing on irrelevant benefits. I was once in the market for public relations services for a new video rollout, only to be sold unneeded SEO services. I was out the door in no time.

Keep in mind that many of your answers will serve as the groundwork for your video script. Your total runtime, most likely, will be around 90 seconds. This length has to cover your introduction and resolution, so you only have around one minute to talk about your product.

- **What is the problem your product addresses?**
  Another way of asking this is, "How do you alleviate your customer's pain?"

- **What are your features and benefits?**
  Hone in on 1-2 things, and be specific.

- **What are your differentiators?**
  What makes you stand out. Again, less is more. Aim for 1-2 things.

- **What are common objections?**
  Or what are your friction points to sale? If you're promoting an idea, or educating, you might consider "objections" as arguments or general resistance to your spiel.

- **Who is your competition, if any?**
  Consider who else is vying for both your audience's money and attention. On the money side, maybe this is a rival company, or an in-house solution. On the attention side, this might be other sites, videos, or everyday distractions. This will help you visualize the viewing context.

- **How do you charge and monetize?**
  If your payment system is convenient, and it's a selling point, you may want to emphasize it. If not, you should still keep this one top of mind because your prospective customers will.

Strategy

Your strategy ties your call to action to your narrative, and for that reason it's so important. In my experience, the strategy questions are the most neglected. By answering them, you'll be miles ahead of most video creators. If you boiled these considerations down, you might think of this as the Why and How.

- **How will your video be distributed?**
  Will it live on your site, YouTube, tradeshows and other events? What initial ideas do you have for getting it out there? No worries if you're drawing a blank; we'll dig into this before long.

- **What is the objective of your video?**
  We covered this earlier, but it's a good idea to put it alongside your other considerations. Remember to focus on what's measurable, like lead generation, sales, user engagement, and brand awareness.

- **What action(s) should your viewer take?**
  Zoom back in on your CTA and incorporate it into your message.

- **How long will your video be?**
  90 seconds is the gold standard for explainers. Longer than that, and there's a direct correlation between runtime and drop-off rate. That being said, your

length will depend on your format and how your video fits your funnel.

Brand

Have you ever landed on a sleek, intelligent-looking homepage for a high-end product, only to find a low-quality stick figure animation? You don't want your video to cut against your brand. Fortunately, you can avoid this pitfall by keeping these points in mind.

- **What is your brand personality?**
  Think about the tone you project. Is it fun, serious, smart, buttoned-up? How much leeway do you have for humor? If most of your blog content is serious and academic, then your video should not be a goofy laugh-fest.

- **What is your brand promise?**
  This is a little more conceptual. Definitionally, from AbuLLard's *Abc's of Branding*, your brand promise is the statement that you make to customers that identifies what they should expect for all interactions with your people, products, services, and company. A great example is Apple: No matter what the interaction, you're promised an aesthetically clean experience.

- **Do you have a visual style?**
  Maybe there are certain colors, shapes, or an overall look you're going for. Think about how your video will match the scenery on your website.

- **Do you have a logo?**
  This one is pretty straightforward. Just make sure you have it ready for your producer, as it will pop up at the end frame. Make sure it's a vector version, which can be edited and expanded without resolution issues (usually this sort of file ends with ".eps" or ".ai").

Audience

Now for the core of the Creative Interview. There are countless examples of marketing materials that fail to address their audience's pain. You probably understand what your customers want. Here's where you'll take a minute to make sure you focus on the facts that matter.

- **What are the demographics of your audience?**
  Is it mostly male or female? What general age range? What education level? These points will affect key decisions, like your voice over artist and characters.

- **What seniority are they?**
  This and the next questions apply primarily to a B2B offering.

- **Do they need buy-in from superiors before they contact or engage you?**
  Is your typical viewer the decision maker? If not, what buy-in is needed from others?

- **What stage of the sales funnel are they in?**
  Keep your sales cycle in mind. Is your typical viewer just getting started on their journey, or will they be ready to sign up right away?

- **What is their mindset when approaching your site?**
  Do they know they have a problem? Do they know what the solution is? Are they just looking for right provider?

Technique

What is a video style that excites you from the get-go?

Don't worry, you don't have to make your final technique choice right now, but it's a good exercise to start thinking of your visual approach as it relates to your Creative Interview considerations. If there's a style you're excited about, here's your chance to reflect on how well it will gel with your product, strategy, brand, and audience.

Customer Development Primer

If you're having trouble answering these questions, don't worry; this quick and dirty crash course on customer development (CD) will help you fill in the blanks.

Customer development is its own book, if not a multitude of texts. Here you'll find basic resources and ideas for answering the important questions about your product and customers.

You've probably started on your customer development journey in one way or another. For background, it's a 4-step process originally developed by entrepreneur and academician Steve Blank. It deals with (A) validating the right market for your idea, (B) building the right product features to solve customer needs, (C) testing the correct model for acquiring and converting customers, and (D) building the right framework for scalability. To boil that down, CD is made up of problem discovery, product discovery, product validation, and scale.

For our purposes, the questions informing your message will apply to the first two steps: problem and product discovery. Validation and scalability are beyond our purposes.

Interviews are a tried and true method for learning about your customers' problems, and figuring out your solution. Here's a play by play for setting up and getting the most out of your interviews.

First, arrange interviews with a good number or your prospective customers — ideally 10 or more. Use LinkedIn as a prospecting tool.

Next, focus on open-ended questions. Here are **problem discovery** questions:

- What are the top 3 challenges you face?
- What are some unmet needs you have?
- What's the hardest part about being . . .?
- What daily tasks take the most time?
- What product do you wish you had?

Next, move on to **product discovery** questions:

- What's appealing to you about our product?
- What deters you from our product?
- What would make this experience better?
- Wave magic wand — how does the solution look?

Here are some great customer development resources:

- **Meetup**
  Go to events, reach out to organizers, post on the forums. Meetup is an ideal network for conducting one-on-one interviews.

- **Craigslist**
  Make and respond to posts related to your industry; solicit interviews.

- **Twitter**
  Search by hashtag for relevant phrases to see what issues and needs your audience is conversing about.

- **BuzzSumo and Quora:**
  We talked about these tools earlier in reference to keyword research. Similarly, use these tools to find (A) the issues or questions your audience is dealing with, and (B) the topics that resonate with them.

Throughout your research, pay close attention to the customer issues that come up repeatedly. Also, keep an eye on phrasing, and incorporate this verbiage into your video. For example, I might choose to emphasize "explainer video" over "product video" after observing that it's used more often.

Takeaways

A video can go anywhere and do anything. Animation in particular has few limits. Regardless of your technique, format, or goal, developing a compelling concept starts by limiting your creative options.

Take some time to clear out the distractions and focus on the easy stuff. These are the considerations you know intimately. Through this process you'll have the groundwork for your video. Later if you choose to write your own script, your narrative will be stronger, and the writing process will be approachable. If you choose to offload scripting to a producer, they will be in a position to carry your message effectively.

Explainer videos can bring multimillion dollar results, but there are many other successful formats that few companies consider. You'll learn about them in the next chapter.

4. Choosing the Right Format

When explainer videos rose to massive prominence, I used get calls and inquiries from all sorts of companies excited about the approach. I heard from plenty of tech startups, B2B software firms, and other complex companies that were primed to achieve stellar results from this asset. But I also fielded leads from real estate brokers, local pizza chains, and purveyors of well-understood consumer products. One example was a company hawking a fall alert system for the elderly, and by their own admission it was identical to the others on the market. These opportunities almost always fizzled out, and before long I began advising certain clients against creating an explainer when I knew it went against their best interests.

So how do you know if an explainer video will be appropriate for your situation? You'll find out in this chapter. Also, you'll get insight into formats that most companies don't consider.

Explainer Videos

Explainers are excellent for handling complexity. Characters, stories, schematics, and symbols combined with a stream of auditory information means projecting a lot of information in a short amount of time. For this reason, the format is a mainstay for tech companies, apps, software, and complex B2B services. Due to the long-term gains, if you're a fit for this tool and you haven't implemented it yet, it should be your top priority.

The keyword here is *explain*, so make sure your product warrants explanation. Educational needs usually start with a new product, feature, or buyer group.

Above all, explainers are made to sell problems. This is pain that your audience may not know they're experiencing until you emphasize it and showcase a better option. For example, a service that let's you search, rate, and hire commercial real estate brokers is probably right for an explainer. If this was your product, you would need to drive home the pain of using traditional classified ads (or whatever) while showcasing your solution. On the other hand, if you're a commercial real estate broker, an explainer serves little purpose. People are familiar with what you do and the pain you solve: finding office space.

This format's sexiness makes it easy to get carried away. To decide if it's the right fit, take a second to scan through the below flow chart.

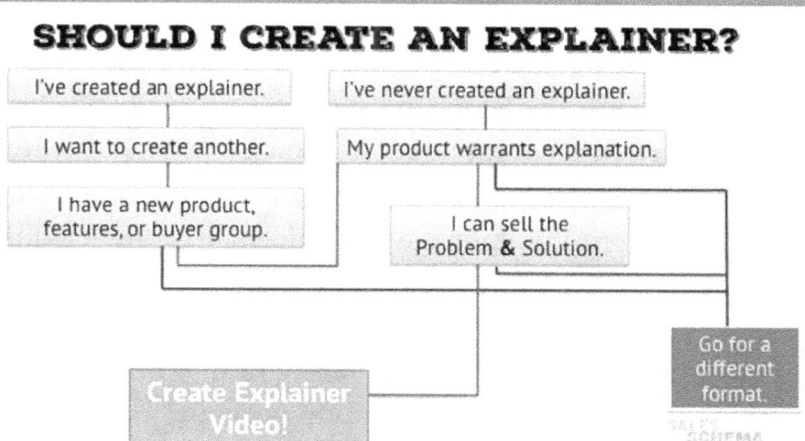

Commercials

There comes a point when complex niches become understood, and an educational element is less necessary. Case in point: apartment-finding services. These companies once relied on educational videos to hold the viewer's hand while selling themselves. Now Jeff Goldblum serves as the promotional face for Apartments.com in 15-second television spots. The niche has arrived.

While explainers are excellent for conversions, lead generation, and sales, commercials are built for more ephemeral goals, like long-term brand awareness. With the previous section in mind, if your offering and customer pain are well-understood, then your mission is getting into people's heads, and you might consider video's classic advertising format, the 15-to-30-second commercial.

Explainers live on the web, while commercials can live on both web and television. The latter entails a higher quality expectation, and thus higher production costs, plus local, regional, or national media spends. Additionally, many producers and voice over talents charge more for broadcast usage. With that in mind, airing on television may be prohibitively expensive. If you don't have a major local or brick-and-mortar component, it probably won't justify the cost.

You often find homepage advertisements projected in the same way as explainers, but the benefits of an ad in this environment are questionable. Homepage video ads can feel superfluous. After all, you've already fulfilled the goal of the commercial when your buyer lands on your company's site. Most successful retailers apply this logic by refraining from playing annoying ads once you're perusing their store. Instead of a homepage commercial, use your ad to bus your audience from other places, like YouTube. On your homepage, think about what would be a better use of real estate. Maybe this is a feature on your most successful product, or a newsletter sign up, for example.

Testimonials

This is a great format for showcasing positive customer feedback. Testimonials are valuable because, at the end of the day, we listen to our friends, family, and colleagues. In fact, it's often said that half of all buying decisions are driven by word of mouth, but few companies act on this phenomenon. Testimonials are the closest you can get to creating your own word of mouth marketing.

I can't say they're particularly bad for any offering, but they're ideal for companies that sell on trust and social validation. Furthermore, this format is ideal if you're all about security, reliability, or interesting customer stories. AirBnB, for one, kills it in this arena. Testimonials are a natural choice for them because they can leverage incredible customer stories. After all, their service helps people book reasonably-priced accommodations in exotic woodland treehouses and chic Manhattan condos.

Here are some tips for creating an awesome testimonial:

- **Solicit feedback carefully**
  Wait until you get consistent positive feedback. Don't force it. If you want to be proactive, collaborate with the people who deal with your customers. Maybe these are your account managers and salespeople. Identify appropriate customers and reach out with a soft ask.

- **Arrange interview**
  Use Google Hangouts or Skype. Ask your customer to wear a dark neutral color, with bright consistent lighting, preferably natural. Make sure to give them all the invite details, and a list of your sample questions. Do a dry run to make sure everything looks and sounds good.

- **Do a question brain dump**
  This stream of consciousness exercise will help you avoid awkward dead spots. Simply write out as many

inquiries as possible and place them into each of the next three categories...

- o **(1) General Questions.**
  You might ask: "How did you get started?" "What does your company do?" "How many employees do you have?"

- o **(2) Industry Questions.**
  After building comfort, you might ask, "What has your experience been like when it comes to hiring new employees [or whatever your niche]?"

- o **(3) Vendor Questions.**
  You might ask: "What were you looking for in a vendor?" "How were you measuring performance?" "What did we do differently?" "What did we do better?"

- ● **Focus on your customer**
  Center your video on them and their journey, not yours. Include your logo and a call to action at the end, but let others do the selling.

To see an awesome example, in **Resources**, check out Message Bus's testimonial from their client, About.me. The video showcases the customer's entire journey. Message Bus chose to focus on one particular experience, which gave them leeway to go into detail and tell About.me's story.

PSAs and Newsjacking

Is there a conversation-starting issue that relates to your offering or target audience? Think hard: Chances are there is a current event, or some other focal point, that's entwined with your product or service. If you have a buzzworthy topic at your disposal, then you might want to create a public service announcement, or a "PSA" for short, also known as *newsjacking*.

If you land on an issue that strikes a nerve, you can get major exposure far beyond normal possibilities. Although going viral is a risky proposition, centering your video on a popular issue is a promising tactic.

To come up with ideas, first understand the 3 C's of a great PSA:
- Current
- Confusing
- Controversial

Your topic should be related to your industry, and should fulfill at least one of the above. If you can check off more than one, even better.

Here are some tips for creating and getting the most out of your *newsjackery*:

- **Narrow your focus**
  Pick something that's important to you, and that will engage your audience. Don't try to combine too many topics.

- **Start with an attention-grabber**
  This might be something humorous, shocking, or an incredible statistic.

- **Back up your facts**
  Use the most current sources, and be sure to cite them.

- **Keep it lively and brief**
  Most successful PSAs maintain a high level of energy throughout the video. Though there are some successful long-form PSAs, shorter is better.

- **Your product = afterthought**
  Sell yourself at the very end. You might do this with a logo screen that says, "Video provided by [you]." If your product has a direct tie-in to the issue, then go for a one-line voice over call to action. Just make sure it's not forced, and that it doesn't detract from the message. For example, it might be, "ACME is familiar with the threat of falling anvils. Learn more on our site."

Check **Resources** for a case study from my experience. At IdeaRocket, we created a newsjacking video on the argument to end software patents. We chose to focus on this topic because it's near and dear to our audience of startups and tech companies. The results were promising: 31K views, a lively discussion in the form of 130+ comments, editorial coverage on tech and economics blogs, and a wider audience that eventually improved our leads. This example will come up again later when you learn about piggybacking.

Culture Videos

My animator friend used to poke fun at the way his peers referred to their vocations. When asked, "What do you do?" most animators respond, "I'm an animator with XYZ Company." My friend's peers working at the prolific studios, however, would say, "I work for Pixar," or, "I work for Dreamworks." Their vocations became their employers.

When it comes to the most iconic companies of our time, culture inspires and attracts talent as well as customers. You can observe this phenomenon with Google, Apple, and a plethora of other hip startups. While achieving *Googleian* cultural perception might be overly ambitious, you can reach for the stars with the help of a culture video.

Your specific goal for this format can vary, but in general it's designed to communicate, educate, and build a relationship. It can be projected at your customers or employees.

To get specific, let's talk about the objectives that lend themselves well to culture videos.

- **Building trust and familiarity**
  This can apply to both prospective customers and employees, although you should not mix groups. Like testimonials, if trust, security, reliability, and other similar qualities are your big selling points, then you might consider a culture video.

- **Creating brand personality**
  Maybe there's something compelling about your brand that acts as a differentiator and value add. Most brands have subtlety and nuance that's difficult to get across without video.

- **Attracting talent**
  Acquiring the right talent can make or break your company, and this undertaking has to happen through a long-term continuous effort. Pay and benefits matter, but creating and promoting an environment

where people want to spend their days is equally, if not more, important.

- **Engagement**
This term is thrown around a lot, and its meaning gets diluted. For our purpose, *engagement* means getting people to take action. All that money you're investing in your employee's gym policy, or that CRM software, is being wasted if they don't use it. Your culture video can inspire and educate people about such things.

Here are some tips for creating the best possible culture video:

- **Be honest.**
Get the most appropriate talent and inspire the right action by creating a genuine message. Don't try to emulate other companies if they don't share your values.

- **Sell on your strengths.**
Focus on the aspects that make your company a great place to work, and stray away from the areas where you're lacking.

- **Speak to your audience.**
Different than a marketing pitch, you can get into the weeds a little bit if it means speaking your audience's language. This is an opportunity to flex your esoteric nerd muscles. If your culture video is meant to recruit software engineers, don't be afraid to talk about SQL Server.

- **Go unconventional.**

  There's no single formula for a great culture video. Some are tongue-in-cheek, others are emotional, and some get very technical. Don't hesitate to break conventions. After all, you're speaking to an inside audience of peers, as well as customers who want to get a feel for the real you.

- **Don't go overboard.**

  If you're a 5-person company, then creating a super-polished culture video might not be a worthwhile investment. Go for a recorded PowerPoint, whitepaper, or an infographic to fulfill your communication needs.

In **Resources,** be sure to check out awesome culture videos from Spotify, Hubspot, and the gaming company Kixeye.

Walkthroughs and Tutorials

Remember that nifty customer funnel from earlier? While explainers will on-board your visitors at the top of your funnel, walkthroughs and tutorials live further down your funnel. These formats will move your leads to the eve of customer-hood. They offer more leeway for a longer runtime because your audience is more engaged than a new visitor. Walkthroughs and tutorials can run from 1 to 30 minutes.

This format works best for complex products (no surprise there). Examples include software and apps, and when it comes to physical products, machinery, or anything where assembly is required.

Walkthroughs work well for products with multiple use cases or buyer groups. For example, maybe you sell a social media monitoring product to brands and ad agencies, and each group uses different features in unique ways.

Here are uses and benefits you can expect from tutorials:

- **Leveraging existing content**
  Maybe you've already written a step-by-step guide on some aspect of your product. Maybe you've made instructions for colleagues or employees. It's pretty straightforward to repurpose this stuff into a customer-facing product tour.

- **Directing users to the right places**
  Videos tours will make sure you show the right message to different buyer groups. For example, if you have an email service like MailChimp, some users might be interested in design and customization, and others in tracking and analytics. With tutorials, you can go in-depth into each.

- **Understanding users**
  Because tutorials let you cover more complexity than explainers, they will let you better understand your users. To make feedback easy, integrate a live chat window or a messaging widget alongside your content.

- **Supporting your FAQ**
  If you have a complex product, there are almost certainly some confusing areas, and that's where a Frequently Asked Questions, or FAQ, page comes in. Product tours will add to the effectiveness, or even take the place, of your FAQ page. The result of

explaining things once in a video means you won't have to repeat yourself over and over when confusion arises. This logic applies to both internal and external audiences.

- **Inexpensive**
  All you need is a computer and a screen capture editing program. The learning curve is relatively small. Camtasia is best for PC, and Screenflow for Mac. These programs are about $100.

Here are tips for creating a great walkthrough or tutorial:

- **Use clear, sequential steps**
  Make sure each step builds off the last one, and that the video brings the viewer to a new level of understanding.

- **Soft sell through demonstration**
  Give your viewers a limited taste of what it's like to use your product. Make signing up the next logical step.

- **Be succinct**
  Brevity is a recurring theme in this book. If there's a complex, lengthy use case you want to demonstrate, see what you can do to condense it to a snappy high-level overview.

- **Keep a clear funnel and call to action**
  Make it obvious what your prospective customer is supposed to do next. Use arrows, buttons, or whatever does the job.

In **Resources** you'll find examples of stellar tutorials and walkthroughs from Hubspot and Wufoo.

Interactive

Imagine if your site's user experience melded with your video. Now mix that with the "choose your own adventure" books of your childhood, and you have interactive video, a cutting-edge approach that's sure to stand out.

Interactive video allows you to click and select different choices within the experience. This means you can tailor different parts of your video to different audiences and interests.

Those are the pros. The main con, and this is a personal pet peeve, is that the format undercuts one of videos main strengths: passivity. A big reason video is compelling is that it lets viewers sit back, relax, be entertained, sometimes while learning something. "Interactive" means work, kind of like you're navigating a site for certain information.

The other challenge is that it requires front-end web development using HTML 5. For that reason, it's ideal for coders, and those ready for at least a minor website redesign. In the production book later, you'll learn about companies that do this sort of work if you'd like to hire it out.

Here are tips for making a powerful interactive video while avoiding major pitfalls:

- **Don't overcomplicate.**
  Limit the number of actions you want your viewers to complete. Use the technology to enhance your message, not muddle it.

- **Make interactivity obvious.**
  Sometimes interactive videos fall flat when it's not clear when or where users are supposed to click. Remember that this technology is relatively new, so you may need to hold your viewer's hand a bit.

Takeaways

I hope this chapter has left you with some cool ideas for your next video. Just to drive this point home, if your offering is a fit for an explainer, then it should be your top priority. When it comes to complex offerings, the format has the most longevity and potential for successful results.

Keep in mind that your format must be selected to fit your goals, not the other way around. Before you get too excited about any particular approach, circle back to your objectives.

If you're like the thousands of companies with whom I've spoken about video marketing, then you're probably wondering how much you should invest in this medium. The best way to find out is to determine your target ROI. You'll learn how in the next chapter.

5. ROI and Measurement

In this chapter, you'll learn the five-step process for finding the target ROI of your video. A big hat tip to Will Gadea from IdeaRocket for providing the process explained here.

Finding target ROI is a valuable exercise, and very few people take the time to do it. It will empower you by letting you know what you can invest in marketing and production. This will help you assign resources, and ultimately achieve the best quality for your budget.

Most unsuccessful campaigns aren't necessarily outright failures. Rather, they fail to meet expectations. This usually happens in the face of vague or unrealistic goals. Many companies think, "We're going to make an amazing video, it will go viral, and we'll be rich!" Instead of falling into that trap, you'll define what success means. You'll aim for a target ROI that's ambitious but attainable.

This exercise is not about being exact or perfect. There will be factors you didn't consider, and real time catch-up. If it's your first go-round with a video campaign, you may miscalculate expected performance, and that's okay. The value comes from creating a baseline that grounds your high-minded goals to specific metrics. This anchor will help you execute.

Though unlikely, maybe you go through this process only to find that video isn't worth the investment at the moment. If you're in this boat, you'll learn about the less resource-intensive alternatives.

Step 1: Identify Your Objective

You should have this in mind from the earlier chapter. If needed, circle back to to it.

You may have multiple goals, but be sure to focus on the one that's most important to your bottom line, and make sure it's measureable.

Step 2: Choose a Metric

Now it's time to assign a metric to your chosen objective. To narrow this down, let's focus on the common objectives from earlier.

- **Sales: Dollars** (or your local currency)

- **User Acquisition: Users** (Hooray for Captain Obvious)

- **Lead Generation: Leads**
  Make sure you have a system in place for tracking leads. This might be a contact form with a "Thank you" page goal destination in Google Analytics, or a custom tracked phone number.

- **Awareness: Mentions, Web Activity**
  There are tons of tools out there for tracking awareness. You can set up Google Alerts for your brand keywords, or you can use social media monitoring tools like Hootsuite, Crowdbooster, and Radian6.

- **Education and Communication = Survey, Quiz Results, et al.**
  This objective carries a few possible metrics. Survey results are telling, but they require a lot of creation and outreach time to get sufficient results. Alternatively, you might choose to embed short quizzes or questionnaires after your video. If the educational effort is customer-facing, then you might choose metrics like those for awareness.

Step 3: Assign a Dollar Value

There are a few moving parts that go along with this one, so bear with me!

Sales

Your dollar value per sale is your *gross profit per sale* (not your revenue). Your gross profit includes all expenses minus your fixed costs. Your fixed costs are those not tied to a sale, like rent and utilities. If you owned a cookie bakery, for example, the cost of dough and chocolate would factor into your gross profit margin, but you would exclude your monthly power and custodial expenses.

Users

If you're an established company, you might know the value of your users based on previous campaigns. If you invest X dollars in your most promising marketing channel, you can expect a Y user increase. This cost would encompass the historic results achieved from investing in ads, your blog, events, trade shows, and other avenues.

On the other hand, maybe you're a startup and you're pursuing funding. You don't have data from which to draw. In this case, you can base your value per user on the funding goal you hope to achieve. For example, if your funding goal is $100,000, and you know you need to bring in 10,000 users in order to validate your product, then your value per user is $10.

Leads

This metric is often more relevant for B2B products and services. To find your value per lead, use this equation:

$$\text{Close Rate} \times \text{Gross Profit Per Sale}$$

Let's look at an example. Jerry is the CMO for an enterprise software product. He talks to his sales team, and they inform him that that they close about 1 in 20 leads, or a close rate of 5%. To get his gross profit per sale, Jerry goes to the CFO of the company. Jerry knows their average deal size is $20,000, and the CFO lets him know that they make 25% gross margin on each sale, or a $5,000 gross profit. Now that Jerry has his close rate and his gross profit per sale, he determines the value per lead at $250...

$$5\% \times \$5,000 = \mathbf{\$250}$$

Awareness

This and the next goal require a bit of guess work. It can be tough to close the loop between broad awareness and actual dollars. That said, if you have the experience and data on hand, you should be able to make a pretty good approximation. Check to see if there has been a correlation between web activity, mentions, or likes, and sales. Average out this increase while being conservative to apply a dollar value to your chosen awareness metric.

Education and Communication

While assigning an exact dollar value is difficult, you should consider the massive effects that can arise from small educational improvements. For example, if your culture video attracts just one awesome job applicant, what might that mean for your bottom line? At IdeaRocket, we created an educational series to prevent workplace accidents at oil drilling sites. If the videos prevent just one serious accident, then our client's investment is justified many times over.

Step 4: Compare Performance

After you've launched your video and you have data, you'll be able to A/B test and compare actual performance. For now, you will use context to find what improvement is attainable. To do this, you'll look at the results from companies related to yours. These might be competitors, partners, or businesses in similar industries. You'll focus on the metric you determined earlier.

So how do you find this data? Start with the low-hanging fruit by looking for published case studies. Try Google's advanced search modifiers. In the below examples, put your specifics in the **bolded** areas.

Plug in a company in the first bracket and your metric in the second. Make sure this is a common keyword, like "sales" or "leads". If you don't have a company in mind, you can do the same search for your industry: for example, "email apps".

[**company**] + "explainer video" + (results OR "case study") OR ([**Metric - leads, sales, etc.**])

[**industry**] + "explainer video" + (results OR "case study") OR ([**Metric - leads, sales, etc.**])

To expand your options, leverage your personal network. Identify peers in related companies who launched video marketing campaigns. If you're coming up empty, lean on

LinkedIn as a prospecting tool. You can use this template if you'd like:

Hi NAME,

I just came across your explainer. Awesome work! I'm considering creating a similar product video, and I was hoping to learn about your experience. I'm curious to know what effect the video has had on lead generation [or whatever your metric].

Do you have time to talk for a few minutes, say, tomorrow 1 to 3 p.m.?

Thanks in advance,

-YOUR NAME

Finally, you can call the studio who created your competitor's video. Their results will be telling. To find the studio, just send your competitor a short note asking who created it (it can be anonymous, or from a pseudonym if you want).

Let the studio know you're considering creating a video like your competitor's. Tell them you're developing your strategy and you're trying to determine if it will be a worthwhile investment. Many producers create case studies on their clients' results, and will be happy to share, especially if it means winning your future business. Regardless, there's no harm in asking.

Make sure your comparison time frame is similar for the companies you're observing. Some businesses enjoy a ton of site traffic and conversions, so they can measure performance in as little as a week or two. For high-end B2B offerings with long sales cycles and low site traffic, it might take months to measure results.

Once you gather your comparison data, ideally from at least a couple different sources, be conservative about it. If you got 75% or even 50% of the results, what would that mean for your bottom line? In the next step, where you calculate ROI, use these more cautious numbers.

Let's see what's new with Jerry: After reaching out to a few related companies and reviewing case studies, he decides that a 20% lead increase is a good target. For Jerry's comparison timeframe of 30 days, this translates to an increase from their current 64 leads to 80, or an additional 16 leads per month.

Step 5: Find ROI

To find your target ROI, start with this equation. Jerry will help us out. . . .

Total value = Value per Metric × Expected Performance
Jerry: \$250/lead × 16 leads = \$4,000

Now that you have found your total value, the next step is finding your *additional* value. To do this, subtract the amount you expect to pay your producer, plus the cost of the time invested by you and your team. You might not have enough information to make a completely informed estimate about producer pricing—don't worry, you'll learn about this in the production book. For now, make a rough guess.

Jerry values his time at \$30/hr and he expects to spend 5 hours on production. The entire project is on his shoulders (poor guy), so there are no hours coming from his team. He estimates he will pay his producer \$2,000, bringing his Total Production Cost to \$3,500.

Total Additional Value = Total Value − Total Production Cost

Jerry: \$500 = \$4,000 − \$3,500

Finally, use this equation to find your Target ROI:

Target ROI = (Total Additional Value ÷ Total Production Cost) × 100

Jerry: **14%** = (\$500 ÷ \$3,500) × 100

Measuring Performance

Now that you've forecasted your target ROI, it's time to set an action plan for measuring actual results. Here is a preparation checklist for making sure you have all your tools ready for performance monitoring.

- **Set up Google Analytics**
  If you're unfamiliar, Google Analytics tracks many aspects of your site's performance. Make sure to track conversions as they apply to the metric you chose earlier. If it's leads, then you might set your conversion goal as the "thank you" page on which users land after submitting a consultation request. G-Analytics is a lot to learn as a whole, but thankfully you don't have be a wizard to keep track of the few important metrics.

- **Get enough data**

  You don't need a huge stream of people, but make sure you have enough traffic to serve as a comparison baseline. If you're a brand new company, don't worry: Before long you will learn strategies for driving traffic with your video. If you're established, then keep track of performance for at least a month before posting your video.

- **Create measurement schedule**

  Select an ideal time frame for comparing results, and set calendar updates. One month will work for many, if not most, products.

- **Record results**

  You can get fancy with marketing automation platforms like Hubspot, or you can use a simple spreadsheet for recording traffic and conversion changes. Although Google Analytics keeps historic data, recording results proactively will ensure you stay on top of your video's performance.

IdeaRocket Results

In the example from our buddy Jerry, you might be wondering if a 20% lead increase is overly ambitious. In my experience, not at all.

At IdeaRocket, there was a period in our early days when we did not practice what we preached. At the beginning of 2012, we had no explainer video on our homepage. After finally adding one, which you can find in **Resources**, we enjoyed a 46% lead increase. For context, we were getting most of our traffic from Google AdWords, and we did almost zero additional marketing when we put up the video. The increase came from the homepage explainer alone.

Video Alternatives

Let's say you plug in all the numbers and you find that video probably is not worth the investment. Or maybe you're just really iffy about it. If you're not ready to take the plunge, here are some accessible alternatives. Since they're highly visual, you can think of them as stepping stones toward video. If they perform well, then it's a sign that you should rethink video in the future.

Prezi

Unlike PowerPoint, Prezi is a giant canvas, and you can pan and zoom around it. It comes with lots of premade templates. When you complete a presentation you can embed it on your site.

Infographics

These are highly shareable and can spread like wildfire. Like explainers, they get a lot of information across in a short amount of time. In line with the newsjacking strategy from earlier, you can expand your exposure by focusing your infographic on a current issue.

SlideShare

Owned by LinkedIn, it's a venue for showcasing PowerPoint-style presentations. It can be a great traffic-driver, and we'll be exploring it in depth in the Strategies, Tools, and Hacks chapter.

DIY Video

Not an alternative, per se, but it's certainly a super-low cost way to get a video. Platforms include PowToon and GoAnimate. The quality level is low, but if that's okay for your brand, it may be worth exploring.

Takeaways

Relax: You're done with the math! The rest of the book is smooth sailing. If you haven't yet, take a second to go through this target ROI exercise. You don't have to reach out to relevant companies for a performance comparison just yet, as that will take some time. For now, just fudge the numbers while being conservative. I think you will enjoy having a baseline in your head, even though you will tweak your estimates as you move forward.

Not all video hosts are created equal. In the next chapter, you will learn what many companies fail to consider when selecting a host.

6. Hosting

While likening one's video to a prized Picasso, I've observed that many companies think of their video host as the painting's frame. As such, their hosting decision is usually an afterthought, leading to dismal results. I've seen too many companies neglect this consideration. They throw their content on YouTube and hope for the best . . . the best rarely happens.

Instead, you should envision your host as the gallery or museum for your masterpiece. Your host creates the context in which your audience experiences your video, and it deserves a bit of strategy. In this chapter, you'll learn what differentiates the top three video hosts, and how to determine which will help you achieve your goals.

YouTube

YouTube is the #2 search engine in the world, after Google. One billion global users traverse it every day. As such, posting a video there can become reflexive.

Your main objective on YouTube should be brand awareness. As such, it's the ideal home for your everyday content videos, which are relatively inexpensive in comparison to a central product explainer and other bigger productions.

Business-centered content videos, like the walkthroughs and tutorials covered earlier, fit perfectly on the world's largest video network. There are probably a ton of topics on which to focus this sort of everyday content. That being said, you might not have the time and resources at your disposal to create these productions at the frequency needed to succeed on this channel.

YouTube's goal is driving traffic to itself. Think of the user-targeted sidebar previews, or how a new video starts playing upon completion of the previous. Given these pull-aways, if you or one of your visitors embeds your YouTube-hosted video elsewhere, there's a high probability that your viewers will end their journey on YouTube.

The network's self-directed strategy makes perfect sense, considering that Google monetizes through in-video ads and static banners. This is supported by Phil Nottingham of Distilled.net. From observing thousands of his clients' business-oriented videos, he found that less than 1 in 100 viewers converted, which would entail migrating from YouTube to an external site. The takeaway here is that the channel is not an ideal traffic driver.

The other factor at work is SEO. Naturally, Google ranks YouTube better than almost any other content. If you host your video on YouTube and on your site with a different host, there's a risk that you'll cannibalize your traffic. When users search for your keywords, company, or explainer, they'll be served the YouTube listing first.

Assuming you're focusing on concrete business goals instead of brand awareness, how do you use YouTube without it using you? Here are a few strategies:

- **Mix up titles and descriptions**
  To get the best of both worlds, you can use YouTube in conjunction with another host embedded exclusively on your site. Just make sure to switch up titles and descriptions between both channels. This will help ensure that YouTube does not gobble up your traffic.

- **Post teasers**
  Use YouTube to feature condensed teaser versions of your high-value content, like your explainer. Drive traffic via a link at the top of your description.

- **Don't seed YouTube links**

   When you're promoting your video to blogs, social media, journalists, or wherever else, make sure to use the link to your video's home on your website and not the YouTube link. Your site is where you'll have the best opportunity to bring visitors into your funnel.

All the risks and warnings aside, you might be wondering how to get the best impact on YouTube, and how to monitor your performance in this space. We'll get into that in the next chapter.

Wistia

You can value Wistia and the next host by what's excluded as much as what's included. Wistia is a straightforward host. There's no network for video sharing, and this means no ads and other attention thieves.

Wistia is business- and marketing-focused. It's centered on helping you leverage video to drive traffic to your website and increase conversions. With that in mind, they give you a ton of analytics. You can see viewer engagement, when dropoffs occur, conversion data, and a lot more.

At the time of this writing, they have four different pricing options. The downside is that to get the bulk of the analytic benefits, you have to shell out $100/month for the "Business" option. They offer a 2-week free trial of this plan if you want to give it a spin.

Their free version has video management tools, and you can upload up to 25 files. The player is branded to Wistia.

Their "Professional" option is the next step up. It's basically the same as the free version, but you can upload up to 100 videos, and the player is unbranded. In addition, there's a high-volume plan that offers expanded bandwidth if you have a ton of files.

Vimeo

Like YouTube, Vimeo features a video sharing network. Unlike YouTube, there are few if any ads and traffic diversions. Vimeo prides itself on being a community of professionals, and it tends to emphasize creatives and artistic projects, although anyone can host there.

As a minor but useful feature, they offer password protection for your videos, so you can share them exclusively with certain people or groups. If you're looking for a solid, stripped-down host, it may be a great fit.

Vimeo has a straightforward, gigabyte-based pricing model at the time of this writing. There's a "Basic" free plan, which allows you up to 500MB per week, which is enough for many companies. The "Plus" plan, at $60/year, gives you more features, and offers up to 5GB/week. The pro plan is $199/year for 20GB/week.

Self-Hosting (Don't Do It)

There are plenty of plugins and software products for self-hosting. I recommend against this route. Here's why:

- **Lack of server bandwidth**
  Video files are huge, and chances are your hosting server won't handle the transmission very well. There's no reason to squander all this time and energy on a terrible viewing experience.

- **Storage limits**
  Most web hosts limit your storage, and big video files can easily tip you over the edge, resulting in overages and slowdowns.

- **Browser issues**
  Different browsers insist on certain file types, like .mp4's or .ogv's. Your video host takes care of this conversion, but sometimes you'll have to handle it if you self-host.

- **No visibility, analytics, other perks . . .**
  Self-hosting means losing the benefits provided by the professionals, like analytics and video management tools.

Takeaways

Make sure to showcase the right content in the right place. If you're going for brand awareness, YouTube is your friend. If you're going for leads, sales, users, or conversions, it's all about your landing page, and YouTube is not necessarily in your corner.

By envisioning the world's largest video network the right way, you're in a stronger position than the many companies that unthinkingly post on YouTube and hope for the best. You'll be able to get the most out of the network without it eating the traffic for which you've worked so hard.

When it comes to hosting, your best move is to leave it to the pros. Thankfully, there are plenty of great platforms, and you won't have to break the bank.

The next chapter will focus on specific steps for driving YouTube results, assuming the network aligns with your goals.

7. YouTube

As you probably know from experience, this one-billion strong network can be a noisy and intimidating place. While it features a world of users, there are a multitude of video creators vying for rankings and audience.

The goal of this chapter is not to make you the next YouTube celebrity. We're not going to get into the vast array of strategies for making connections and building a YouTube brand.

The neverending marketing options that this network entails makes it easy to get overwhelmed and lose sight of what's important. If you have an emerging product or service, I'll go out on a limb by guessing that funding, sales, leads, and users are more important to you than YouTube views and subscribers.

With all this in mind, we'll take a low-maintenance, bang-for-your-buck approach to the network. You'll focus on the areas that are most likely to affect your impact on this channel.

Titles and Tags

The first elements are your titles and tags. While this is geared toward YouTube, the exercise can be applied to naming your video wherever it lives. Furthermore, this process will lend itself well to naming blog posts and other content.

To source the most relevant title, circle back to your keyword research. You might want to revisit Google Trends, focusing your search on YouTube exclusively (simply check the corresponding box). From there, write out 10-15 titles, and the best couple should jump out at you. If you're on the fence about your title, know that you can change it later and A/B test if you'd like.

Make sure to use your primary keyword at the beginning of your title phrase. Don't be afraid to use your KW multiple times, as long as it looks natural. Base your title on common problems and questions users are expressing on YouTube. Above all, it should match the way people search.

For insight, this is a strong title: "Video Marketing Ideas for Startups"

This is a weak title: "How to Get the Most Out of Your Video Marketing Strategy"

Very few people would search with a phrase like the latter. Yet, it's the sort of name you see all the time.

As a specific hint, if appropriate, go with a "How to . . ." title, like, "How to Use Video Marketing for Your Startup." As noted by Search Engine Land, searches with this lead-in increased more than 70% on YouTube, based on 100 million hours watched in 2015.

Descriptions

Descriptions are an important ranking factor because YouTube, and search engines in general, can't crawl your videos in a detailed way. On YouTube, you have around 500 words to work with, so you might as well use your real estate. With that in mind, you should envision your description like a blog post.

You might be worried that this will be a ton of extra work, but it doesn't have to be. Your description can be a slightly adapted video transcription. In the next chapter, you'll learn about a quick and easy service for creating this asset.

Another huge benefit of a detailed description is that it will let you rank for long-tail keywords. As defined by WordStream, long-tail keywords are longer and more specific phrases that visitors are more likely to use when they're closer to a point-of-purchase. Since they're less common, there's less competition in the search engine. As a result, your product will appear at or near the top of search results when a user searches for those keywords. For example, "video marketing" would be my primary keyword, but "video marketing for startups" or "video marketing on a limited budget" might be my long-tails. To inspire these phrases, check out SEO Chat's "Google Keyword Suggest" tool, which you'll find in **Resources**.

Make sure to include the link for your video's call to action at the very top of your description. If you mentioned any other sites or sources, make sure to link them as well. This can be a great way to build links and relationships.

Thumbnails

Your thumbnail is like a glossy movie theater poster promoting this summer's next blockbuster. The same rules apply: You want something intriguing and memorable.

If you're in the live action camp, it's been found that featuring a human face will attract the most views. Overall, make it stand out. It should be poignant and compelling so it will win over competing search results.

Consider the colors you're up against. If the results are weighted towards greys and whites, use a bright scheme, and vice versa. Simply adding a colorful border frame can make your thumbnail pop. Also, consider incorporating large and concise text, and include your primary keyword.

YouTube KPIs

We talked about how YouTube should be geared toward brand awareness. Going further, this means catering to your relevant audience, usually a subset of your video's entire viewership. These targeted viewers are at the start of their path towards becoming customers.

If going viral is not a reasonable goal, how do you develop concrete Key Performance Indicators, or KPIs, for this channel?

Phil Nottingham of Distilled.net provides a helpful process for calculating the number of engaged users in your demographic. As he notes, views alone aren't worth much without understanding context: who was viewing, how long they viewed, bounce rate, and other factors.

One of the most valuable KPIs is *Engaged Views*. To understand what this metric encompasses, look to this formula:

Engaged views = Number of Views × Average Percentage Viewed [*i.e., 30 sec of 1-min video=50%*] × Demographic Viewer Percentage

To fill in these variables, check out YouTube's Analytics section. You'll need to download and combine data from relevant .CSV reports in Excel. This involves moving around some numbers because YouTube doesn't automatically provide this level of detail. To learn how to do this, check out Phil's article ("Metrics to Measure YouTube Marketing"), Linkedin **Resources**.

Let's zoom forward and look at an example. Let's say your demographic is American females, aged 20-35. This is your starting place.

Your total view count is 100,000. Next, you check out the "Audience Retention" report and find that viewers watch 80% of your video on average, or 1:36 of 2 minutes. Next, you find that 70% of your total viewers fit your target demographic. Now let's combine everything:

Views: 100,000

Average Percentage Viewed: 80%

Demographic Viewer Percentage: 70%

$100,000 \times 0.80 \times 0.70 = 56,000$

This number indicates that you have 56,000 engaged users in your demographic. This insight is much more relevant to your bottom line than views alone.

Takeaways

Remember when I said that video should be part of your marketing strategy, not the other way around? When you read that, maybe it seemed like an obvious point. When it comes to the world's largest video network, however, it's easy to spin your wheels and misprioritize objectives that won't have much impact on your bottom line.

I don't want to downplay YouTube's value. Instead, I want to encourage you to think of it as a useful tool for achieving your goals instead of envisioning it as the goal unto itself. To get the most out of this channel, devoting a little upfront work to your titles, tags, descriptions, and thumbnails will give you the best performance for the least amount of effort. As always, tie these elements back to your goals and vision, including your keyword research and the Creative Interview.

In the next chapter, we're going to get nitty and gritty. You'll learn simple and specific actions for generating traffic and conversions from your video.

8. Strategies, Tools, and Hacks

You might be yelling into your book or tablet: "Okay Dan, I understand the conceptual mumbo-jumbo now. How are you going to help me land more sales and conversions? How will you help me bring home the bacon?!"

Calm down, put your shirt back on, and put down the hammer. This chapter is where you'll learn specific strategies, tools, and hacks for getting results.

As usual, you'll use video as a powerful enhancement to your overall marketing push. The objective is not getting people to your video, but using your video to get people to your objective.

Transcriptions

We've covered video's SEO value. Google prioritizes the medium over almost any other content. Although search engines can parse it, they aren't smart enough to digest the details.

To make things easy for your robot friends, create a video transcription. A transcription is simply the written version of your video, although you don't necessarily have to transpose all the words verbatim from your audio track.

Often you see transcriptions embedded within the video as captions. This offers SEO benefits, since Google can indeed crawl them, as well as advantages for getting your message across to hearing-impaired viewers and those facing language barriers.

To take transcriptions to the next level, however, you should use them as an accompanying blog post. In addition to the communication benefits, this will aid viewers who might prefer text over audio and visuals; some will be out and about, or in noisy environments. Incorporating your transcript into a blog post below the fold will let you cater to all viewing situations.

Don't take my word for it; just check out Moz, the foremost SEO authority after Google. For founder Rand Fishkin's "Whiteboard Friday" series, the company includes a textual blog-like transcript right below the video, which is positioned appropriately as the hero. Head over to **Resources** to check it out.

To create easy transcipts, Speechpad.com is a super sleek and automated option. They charge $1/minute, which comes to just a few bucks for most videos. If you need the transcript synced to the video's timing, most services charge around $1.50/minute.

As a side note, Moz uses Wistia when hosting "Whiteboard Fridays" and other content on their site. Rand noted that they will often post the same content on YouTube, but will switch up titles, descriptions, and other metadata so that their traffic is not cannibalized.

Video Sitemaps

Creating and installing a video sitemap is a quick and easy way to boost your SEO by showing Google how to find and crawl your videos. When you improve your findability, you can improve your rankings.

If you're on Wistia, there's a sitemap tool as part of their SEO suite. If you have just have a few videos and you don't plan on creating many more, you can probably get away with creating your own sitemap using a tool like the one offered at XML.SiteMaps.com. On Wordpress, the Yoast SEO plugin is excellent, and they offer a paid video SEO extension, and you're doing more than a few vids, it's probably worth it.

Email Video Blasts

55% of marketers report higher click-through rates from emails sent with video than without. If you have a list of subscribers, video can be a great way to move them toward a desired action.

A common question is: "Can you stream video in email?" The answer: Sort of. Some email services allow streaming, and others don't. Outlook and Gmail, two of the biggest, do not. With that in mind, you have to be creative and simulate streaming without actually doing it.

Here's how to set up your video blast:

1. Create a thumbnail that mimics the look of the video player and includes a memorable scene. You can do this by taking a screenshot of your player.

2. Link the thumbnail to your landing page. This is important because many marketers direct email traffic to YouTube or another host. Your audience should migrate to your site so you can start moving them into your funnel.

3. Once they go to your landing page, make sure the video is on autoplay. Under normal circumstances, autoplay might be kind of annoying, but this functionality makes sense in this case because they will have already clicked the player image. If you'd like, you can lead people to a custom landing page just for email traffic.

    To create custom landing pages for different audiences, try OptimizePress or LeadPages. If landing pages won't be an ongoing thing, I recommend the former because it's a one-time fee instead of a monthly commitment.

4. Include "video" in the subject line, which has been found to increase open rates. Your messaging will depend on your product, but in general, keep it conversational and build excitement.

Check **Resources** to see an example of an excellent video email blast from Vidyard, an enterprise video marketing solution. They know their stuff.

Cold Email Campaigns

If you're doing lead generation or sales for a B2B product or service, video is an excellent hook. That said, it all starts with a great cold email. For inspiration, check **Resources** where I've linked a library of hundreds of templates. As these examples will demonstrate, it's better to go for short and conversational instead of a lengthy sales pitch.

Let's check out an example, and then you'll learn about the ingredients that go into it:

Hi PROSPECT,

I'm Dan and I'm Senior Account Manager at IdeaRocket. We create animated marketing videos for increasing leads and sales.

Since we've worked with a few companies like yours (Company A and Company B), I'm wondering, what are you guys doing when it comes to video marketing?

Best,
Dan

PS: to learn more about us, check out **our explainer video [Hypertext Link]**.

Toward the end of your message, there comes a time to explain what you're all about. In a bad pitch, this is usually when the reader bails. If it's lengthy and boring, that is.

Instead of telling your company's life story, use this as an opportunity to entice your reader with your video. The other benefit is brevity: Your short message is more likely to be read and acted upon. Like in your email blast, make the video autoplay when readers land on it.

Here's where the hack comes in: Track your link using email technology like YesWare. For background, apps like this link up to your email platform, and they let you know when your messages are opened and clicked. Because your link will be small and toward the end of your email, you'll know that if it's clicked, your message was probably read. Furthermore, you'll know that your prospect visited your site. This means your cold lead is now quite warm, so don't be afraid to give him or her a call!

Press Booster

Is it time to get your product some PR? Even one or two placements on moderately-trafficked news sites or blogs might mean the difference between millions of users, or funding dollars for that matter. Being able to link to press coverage will give you major social validation that will make just about any other marketing goal much more attainable.

If you hear one major complaint from journalists, it's that they get annoyed trying to understand the companies pitching them. Considering that they're sent hundreds of coverage requests every day, they're likely to trash your message if they don't get what you do right away. For this reason, product videos are now more than a plus: they're an expectation.

Here's the path for using your video to get the most coverage in the shortest time:

1. **Create a list of influential blogs**
   Search for relevant topics in your field in Google under the "News" tab. Also, you can use BuzzSumo, as covered earlier. A third tool is AllTop.com, which categorizes the most popular news sites and blogs by industry.
   Put your research into an Excel or Google Spreadsheet. The latter is preferable because you'll be sharing it, as per the next step. Include columns for site, URL, journalist name, and his/her email.

2. **Hire out research**
   Once you've identified your targets, hire out email address research. Depending on the site, these details might be easy to find, or they might take some detective skills. Thankfully this type of research is one of the most common skills touted by freelancers on Fiverr, Upwork, Mechanical Turk and other hiring networks. A job like this should take around three hours or less, and you'll most likely pay around $5 per hour. If this sort of project will be a one-off, then use Fiverr, and if you're looking for a continuing freelancer relationship, then go with Upwork.

3. Craft your pitch

Revisit the above cold email strategy, but make video a little more prominent. Let your explainer do the talking instead of your text. Here's an example:

Hi [NAME],

I've read several of your articles on [your industry], and I'm a fan. I'll get right to the point: I'm curious if you'd be interested in doing a story on us.

I'm with [your company] and we [your value proposition]. You can learn more from our **explainer video** [LINK].

A feature on [site] would be a huge win for us, and I look forward to hearing your ' thoughts.

Cheers!
-[Your name]

---

4. Blast your message with mail merge software

Using a mail merge platform, you can fill in the custom fields with spreadsheet information, and send hundreds of customized emails. We won't get too far into the technical weeds, but if you're interested in learning more, check out the links in **Resources**. There I've covered a couple tools: a Google app that links up to your spreadsheet, and Mandrill, a transactional email product by MailChimp.

Piggybacking

What if Seth Godin, Guy Kawasaki, and Peter Thiel could propel your product to success? Guess what: The thought leaders in your industry are probably more accessible than you think, especially if you offer them value.

At IdeaRocket, we wanted to build awareness with our target audience of tech startups. So we teamed up with relevant celebrities in our field, based on the topics we found interesting, which we knew would resonate with startups (check these out in **Resources**).

When we approached these thought leaders, we were virtually unknown. Our only bargaining chip was our willingness to create a mutually beneficial video. We offered up no money or other handouts.

For the first, we worked with startup guru and famed robot dinosaur Fakegrimlock to animate his "Minimum Viable Personality" presentation. For the second, we joined forces with economics professor and co-editor of *Marginal Revolution* Alex Tabarrok. We created an editorial video educating viewers about the argument to end software patents, and it included a mischievous Jeff Bezos. The results were stellar: Both got coverage on relevant blogs; the "End Software Patents" video went viral in our niche, garnering over 31,000 views and a lively discussion in the form of 130+ comments. Since the goal was awareness, the exact ROI is difficult to track, but numerous prospects and customers referenced the videos on sales calls, so I'm confident that these campaigns moved the needle.

If you're looking for a fresh idea, piggybacking is a great one. If you decided earlier that an explainer is your best move, then do that first, and keep this in mind for future reference.

Here are some tips for making piggybacking work:

- **Find the right thought leader**
  Focus on someone who gets a lot of attention or readership in your niche. Set your sights high.

- **Find the right content**
  Look for a presentation, speech, article, or some other successful content created by your thought leader that would lend itself well to video. Focus on articles that racked up a lot of views and comments, but still have the potential for a larger audience.

  Like we talked about in reference to PSA videos, prioritize concepts that are current, confusing, and/or controversial. Humor never hurts either.

  The added benefit is that scripting will be much easier if you can draw from an existing presentation.

- **Reach out, get promotional agreement**
  Make sure that your thought leader is 100% on board before you invest any time.

  Lead your pitch with the benefits your celeb will receive: a free video, promotion for forthcoming rollouts, growing their personal brand, etc. Keep in mind that your thought leader might need to promote a book, product, or another initiative. With that in mind, you should consider timing your pitch around an upcoming release.

Make it clear that the time obligation will be minimal, and the cost will be zero. Set expectations about the production obligations (more on this next).

Depending on your needs and your thought leader, the benefit you receive may vary. Generally, you should ask for at least one blog post and several social media messages. To make their life easier, offer to draft this messaging for your thought leader's review.

- **Keep them in the loop**
  While respecting your thought leader's time, make sure to get their approval on key drafts so they can feel comfortable with the trajectory of the video. This usually means showing him or her the script, storyboard, and final drafts.

- **Set expectations about voice over**
  The biggest obligation from your thought leader will be voicing the approved script, for which they will need a decent microphone and a quiet place. They can use free software like Audacity and send you the audio files. In my experience, most people have fun recording voice overs, assuming they're not tech luddites.

- **Include brand end frames and a soft call to action**
  Make sure your video is entirely non-salesy until the end frames, where you drop both your and your thought leader's branding. If your company has a

direct tie-in with the topic at hand, then you might be able to get away with a soft call to action. But don't push it.

Quora

We talked about using Quora as a customer development tool. It's also a great place for driving high-quality traffic to your site, while using video to increase your impact. I've observed greater conversions from users originating from this channel. This is not surprising since it's users are usually dealing with a problem.

To refresh, Quora is a sophisticated question and answer site. There are probably a ton of confusing topics tied to your product's value proposition, and Quora gives you the opportunity to shed light on them.

When you answer questions, focus on being helpful and comprehensive. If you spend a few minutes perusing this network, you'll see that the most complete and educational answers get upvoted and enjoy the greatest prominence. You might include a small promotional angle as an afterthought, like, "By the way, we help companies with this. This video will tell you more. . . ."

When you link your video it will show up as a big thumbnail. This acts like a billboard, and it will add serious real estate to your post.

To get started on Quora, see what people are talking about in your industry. Questions often arise along the lines of, "What are some good examples of explainer video companies [or whatever your niche]?"

To streamline research in this space, set up Google Alerts to tell you when your keywords arise in questions and conversations on Quora. In G-Alerts, simply plug in "site:Quora + [your keywords]".

Distribution Platforms

What if you could instantly seed your video to major hubs like YouTube and Vimeo, as well as dozens of other sharing networks? Enter the video distribution platform, a lesser-known tool that will help you maximize exposure with minimal effort. Putting everything in one place for easy mass uploading can mean major SEO and traffic benefits.

There are a few major distribution platforms, but the leader is OneLoad. The software allows you post to many sites while customizing metadata for each. This can really cut down on navigation and data entry time if you plan on seeding your video to locations like Twitter, Facebook, Tumblr, or Hulu. In addition, you'll get access to networks like Veoh and Dailymotion. Another handy feature is their "global video takedown," which allows you to remove your video from any or all sites at once, instead of going through the tedious process of deleting it over and over.

Repurposing for SlideShare

SlideShare combines the engagement of multimedia with the SEO benefits of crawlable text. Plus, the network gets something like 60 million unique users per month, so there's a ton of traffic to be had.

For background, SlideShare is a LinkedIn-owned network for showcasing PowerPoint-style presentations. Once you have a video, the process of repurposing it for SlideShare is relatively straightforward. Since you will have created a visually engaging piece, you're primed to create a strong presentation.

Here are tips for repurposing your video for SlideShare:

- **Create a system**
  Maybe this is "11 steps for better email marketing", or "5 common problems solved by new apps".

- **Keep it simple**
  If you're speaking to multiple buyer groups, or you have a complex offering, don't be afraid to break the information into two or more presentations.

- **Condense into an outline**
  Aim for 15-30 slides, which is the normal range for successful presentations. Your outline can just be three columns for slide title, visual description, and textual description.

- **Bring key frames into PowerPoint**
  Request the Photoshop (PSD) files from your video producer. Without getting too technical, you'll need to convert these to still frames that you can bring into a presentation platform like PowerPoint or Keynote. Pull out the frames that correspond to the scenes you identified in your outline.

- **Add text**
  Once you have your visuals laid out, add in big blocky text, and make sure it's not competing for attention with your video frames. It often helps to intersperse the vibrant images from your video with solid-colored frames and simple text.

- **Send traffic to your site**
  Early in your presentation (i.e., page 2 or 3), include a slide that drives traffic to your video page. It can be as simple as this:

  "Want to see a video of this presentation? Click here!"

  Make sure to include this link and any other important destinations at the top of the presentation's description.

Trade Shows

If trade show marketing is part of your strategy, here are some big considerations when it comes to your video.

- **Be visually engaging**
  This is always true, but it's especially important when it comes to trade shows, where there's eye candy at every corner. Consider the styles that would make you stop in your tracks from twenty feet away, in the middle of a busy event floor. Keep your video on loop, envisioning it as a Times Square digital billboard.

- **Stay away from audio**
  While going soundless is a bad idea most of the time, a trade show leaves no other choice. The noisy environment will make it difficult to hear voices, music, or sound effects. With that in mind, dynamic text, or kinetic typography, is often an excellent style for this space.

- **Go for the quick hook**

  You don't need to tell your life story; you just need to bring attendees to your booth. Once you're in a conversation, you can sell and educate as needed.

- **Include a real-life call to action**

  Offer a white paper, ebook, or some other helpful asset, and make your video direct viewers to it.

Takeaways

To hammer it home, video is a powerful enhancement, but not the end goal of your marketing. Keep that in mind as you move forward with these strategies. If there's a current marketing channel that's paying off for you, consider how video might make it more powerful. There's no need to reinvent the wheel. Above all, remember that your objective is not to drive people to your video, but rather to drive people to your objective.

If any chapter is dynamic, it's the one you just completed. Everyday, companies are leveraging new networks and techniques for driving traffic and sales. With that in mind, make sure to sign up for the newsletter so I can keep you up to speed on new and compelling video strategies.

9. Producing Your Video

We've covered how newly-launched startups have made upwards of $50 million in a few days from the simple act of adding a homepage explainer. But not all product videos are created equal. Because companies are constantly adding to this medium, it's more important than ever to stand out and leave a lasting impression on your audience.

- So how do you create something memorable?
- How do you make sure your video will convert?
- How do you find the right balance between quality and cost?
- How do you pick the right technique?
- How do you select the right producer?
- How do you write a powerful script?

We'll answer all these questions and many more in the companion book:

The Lean Explainer Video
A Video Production Handbook for Startups and Entrepreneurs

For more details, head to Amazon via this shortlink: **SalesSchema.com/DanAuthorPage**

Key Takeaways

Video can be your strongest marketing asset, or it can be a headache-inducing money pit. It's tempting to rush into production, but you'll save a ton of time, money, and energy by planning and making your strategy gel with your offering.

This means identifying your specific objectives, including your target ROI. Once you go on the market for a producer, you'll find that prices vary tremendously. Knowing how much quality you can afford will be empowering.

You might choose to create an explainer, or a different format like a testimonial or a PSA. Regardless, your approach should be grounded by a guiding vision and specific aims. From there, scale back your natural inclination to create a video for you and your colleagues. Instead, focus on your audience. Hone in on the points you know like the back of your hand. Use the Creative Interview as the foundation for your script.

Understand that not every host is right for all goals. YouTube can get your message to a ton of people, but it's not so great for driving traffic and conversions. Instead, you might consider a host like Wistia or Vimeo, which generally keep your audience on your site.

You learned specific strategies for using video as a powerful marketing enhancer, not a goal unto itself. This is the chapter that will grow and change with technology and experimentation. To keep up to speed, stay tuned to the newsletter and resources page.

With this book, I hope I've given you the tools you need to get results. I hope you land more users, leads, press coverage, funding, or whatever it is you're pursuing. Until next time!

Would you do me a solid?

If you found this book helpful, it would be awesome if you would post a short review on Amazon. You'll be helping future readers know what to expect.

Go here, then select the book:
SalesSchema.com/DanAuthorPage

Thanks in advance!

Special Thanks

This book was made possible through the insight and experience of Will Gadea and the IdeaRocket team. They're the best in the game.

Check out their portfolio at **IdeaRocketAnimation.com**.

About the Author

Dan Englander is a New York-based author and entrepreneur. As the first employee and Senior Account Manager, Dan helped launch IdeaRocket, the premier studio for high-quality animated explainer videos. He brought in business and managed productions for Fortune 500s and startups like Venmo.

He's the founder of Sales Schema, a site that helps companies win by melding sales and digital marketing. He's the author of *Mastering Account Management* and other business books. In addition, he teaches high-level online courses on B2B sales and marketing.

Previously, Dan was Account Coordinator at DXagency, where he increased digital exposure for clients like Monster Cable and Marc Ecko. He's a decent living room guitarist and he makes a mean paella.